Caught in the Trembling Net

Caught in the Trembling Net

Poems by

Karen George

© 2024 Karen George. All rights reserved.
This material may not be reproduced in any form, published,
reprinted, recorded, performed, broadcast,
rewritten, or redistributed without
the explicit permission of Karen George.
All such actions are strictly prohibited by law.

Cover design by Shay Culligan
Cover image by Wyxina Tresse
Author photo by Karen George

ISBN: 978-1-63980-630-0

Kelsay Books
502 South 1040 East, A-119
American Fork, Utah 84003
Kelsaybooks.com

*To my mother Vivian,
my father Joseph,
my husbands Lou and Richard,
who have all passed,
but continue to nourish me in dreams.*

Acknowledgments

Thank you to the editors of the following journals and blogs in which versions of these poems have appeared.

Charge Magazine: "What You Dread"
Ekphrastic Review: "Emily Carr's *Guyasdom's D'Sonoqua*, 1930," "Emily Carr, *Forest, British Columbia*," "Georgia O'Keeffe's *Nude Series III*, 1917," "Georgia O'Keeffe's *Pattern of Leaves*, 1923–4*,*" "Frida Kahlo's *The Dream, (The Bed)*, 1940"
Gulf Stream Magazine: "Georgia O'Keeffe's *Blue No. II*, 1916," "Georgia O'Keeffe's *Blue No. 1*, 1916," "Georgia O'Keeffe's *Red and Orange Streak*, 1919"
Gyroscope Review: "Georgia O'Keeffe's *Lake George with Crows*, 1921," "Georgia O'Keeffe's *Dead Cottonwood Tree, Abiquiu*, 1943"
Juniper, A Poetry Journal: "Emily Carr, *Sombreness Sunlit*"
Lexington Poetry Month blog: "Colour is tangible," "Voluminous," "When one is listening intensely," "I Want To Have My Share," "I Want So terribly To Feel," "To wrestle something out for myself," "Emily Carr, *Laughing Forest*, 1939," "Georgia O'Keeffe's *Evening Star No. V*, 1917," "Georgia O'Keeffe's *The Old Maple, Lake George*, 1926," "There is so little known about," "Listen to Me," "I Have Wanted to Explain to You," "Tell me if you're still learning," "The Enormous Spine of the Imagination"
MacQueen's Quinterly: "Emily Carr, *Scorned Timber, Beloved of the Sky*," "Emily Carr's *The Great Eagle, Skidegate, B.C.*, 1929"
Main Street Rag: "Georgia O'Keeffe's *Blue and Green Music*, 1919"
Mezzo Cammin: An Online Journal of Formalist Poetry by Women: "Frida Kahlo, *The Two Fridas*, 1939," "Is It True?"
Mom Egg Review: "Frida Kahlo's *My Nurse and I*, 1937"

OyeDrum: "Emily Carr's *Zunoqua of the Cat Village,* 1931"
Panoply: "Georgia O'Keeffe's *Summer Days,* 1936"
Persimmon Tree: "Frida Kahlo's *The Love Embrace of the Universe,* 1949"
Salamander: "Georgia O'Keeffe, *Red and Brown Leaves,* 1925"
Sheila-Na-Gig Online: "Georgia O'Keeffe's *Zinnias,* 1921," "Georgia O'Keeffe's *Pelvis III,* 1944," "Georgia O'Keeffe's *Special No. 12,* 1917"
South Broadway Ghost Society: "Frida Kahlo's *The Wounded Deer,* 1946"
Star 82 Review: "Inscription in *Frida Kahlo's Masterpieces,* Half Priced Books"
TAB: The Journal of Poetry & Poetics: "Georgia O'Keeffe's *Two Jimson Weeds,* 1938," "Frida Kahlo, *Henry Ford Hospital, The Flying Bed,* 1932"
Thimble Magazine: "Georgia O'Keeffe's *At the Rodeo, New Mexico,* 1929," "Georgia O'Keeffe's *Series I, No. 8,* 1919"
Thirteen Myna Birds: "Georgia O'Keeffe's *Light Coming on the Plains III,* 1917"
Writing In a Woman's Voice: "Georgia O'Keeffe's *It Was Red and Pink,* 1959," "Frida Kahlo, *Self Portrait with Necklace of Thorns and Hummingbird,* 1940"

I want to thank the following who inspire and support my work: Donelle Dreese, Nancy Jentsch, Taunja Thomson, and members of The Greater Cincinnati Writers League and Cincinnati Writers Project.

Contents

I. Map of Rivery Fissures Frida Kahlo 1907–1954

To Risk the Whole Thing	19
Frida Kahlo's *Henry Ford Hospital (The Flying Bed)*, 1932	20
Frida Kahlo's *Memory*, 1937	21
Frida Kahlo's *My Nurse and I*, 1937	22
Frida Kahlo, *The Two Fridas*, 1939	23
What You Dread	24
I'm Starting to Get Used to Suffering	25
Frida Kahlo's *The Dream, (The Bed)*, 1940	26
Frida Kahlo's *Self Portrait with Necklace of Thorns and Hummingbird*, 1940	27
Frida Kahlo's *The Broken Column*, 1944	28
There is so little known about	30
Frida Kahlo's *Without Hope*, 1945	31
Frida Kahlo's *The Wounded Deer*, 1946	32
Colour is tangible	33
Frida Kahlo's *Tree of Hope*, 1946	34
Inscription in *Frida Kahlo's Masterpieces,* Half Priced Books	35
Listen to Me	36
Frida Kahlo's *The Love Embrace of the Universe*, 1949	37
I Have Wanted to Explain to You	38
Frida Kahlo's *Watermelons,* 1954	39
Tell me if you're still learning	40
After Reading Frida's Letter to Georgia O'Keeffe, March 1, 1933	41

II. Scar Beauty, Inflame It Georgia O'Keeffe   1887–1986

Here I am again	45
Voluminous	47
Georgia O'Keeffe's *Blue No. 1,* 1916	48
Georgia O'Keeffe's *Blue No. II,* Watercolor, 1916	49
Georgia O'Keeffe's *Nude Series VIII,* Watercolor, 1917	50
Georgia O'Keeffe's *Light Coming on the Plains III,* Watercolor, 1917	51
Georgia O'Keeffe's *Evening Star No. V,* 1917	52
Georgia O'Keeffe's *Special #12,* 1917	54
Georgia O'Keeffe's *Blue and Green Music,* 1919	56
Georgia O'Keeffe's *Series I, No. 8,* 1919	57
Today I want to paint nakedness	58
Georgia O'Keeffe's *Red and Orange Streak,* 1919	59
Georgia O'Keeffe's *Zinnias,* 1921	61
Georgia O'Keeffe's *Lake George with Crows,* 1921	62
Georgia O'Keeffe's *Pattern of Leaves or Leaf Motif #3,* 1923–4	63
Georgia O'Keeffe's *New York with Moon,* 1925	64
Georgia O'Keeffe's *Red and Brown Leaves,* 1925	65
Georgia O'Keeffe's *The Old Maple, Lake George,* 1926	66
Georgia O'Keeffe's *The Lawrence Tree,* 1929	67
Georgia O'Keeffe's *At the Rodeo, New Mexico,* 1929	69
Georgia O'Keeffe's *Jack-in-the-Pulpit II,* 1930	71
Georgia O'Keeffe's *Summer Days,* 1936	72
Georgia O'Keeffe's *Two Jimson Weeds,* 1938	73
Georgia O'Keeffe's *Dead Cottonwood Tree, Abiquiu,* 1943	74

Is It True?	75
Georgia O'Keeffe's *Pelvis III*, 1944	77
Georgia O'Keeffe's *It Was Red and Pink*, 1959	78
Georgia O'Keeffe's *It Was Blue and Green*, 1960	79
Living Is Such a Tangle	80

III. Wild Convergence Emily Carr 1871–1945

When one is listening intensely	85
Emily Carr's *War Canoes, Alert Bay*, 1912	86
Emily Carr's *Totem Mother, Kitwancool*, 1928	87
Emily Carr's *The Great Eagle, Skidegate, B.C.*, 1929	88
Emily Carr's Untitled *[Eye in the Forest]*, 1929–30, Charcoal on Paper	89
Emily Carr's *Zunoqua of the Cat Village*, 1931	90
Emily Carr's *Big Raven*, 1931	91
To Wrestle Something Out for Myself	92
Emily Carr's *Forest, British Columbia*, 1931–2	93
Emily Carr's *Gray*, 1931–32	95
Emily Carr's *Abstract Tree Forms*, 1931–32	96
Emily Carr's *Scorned as Timber, Beloved of the Sky*, 1932–35	97
Emily Carr's *Wood Interior*, 1932–35	98
I Want to Have My Share	99
Emily Carr's *Forest Interior in Shafts of Light*, 1935–37	100
Emily Carr's *Reforestation*, 1936	101
Emily Carr's *Roots*, 1937–39	102
Emily Carr's *Sombreness Sunlit*, 1938–40	103
I Want So Terribly to Feel	104
Emily Carr's *Laughing Forest*, 1939	105
Emily Carr's *Self-Portrait*, 1938–39	106
What Is It You Are Struggling For?	107
The enormous spine of the imagination	109

I am not sick. I am broken. But I am happy as long as I can paint.
—Frida Kahlo

To create one's world in any of the arts takes courage.
—Georgia O'Keeffe

*I made myself an envelope into which I could thrust my work deep,
lick the flap, seal it from everybody.*
—Emily Carr

I.

Map of Rivery Fissures

Frida Kahlo
1907–1954

Passion is the bridge that takes you from pain to change.

To Risk the Whole Thing

I've started to paint the intense experience
of only painful things
the wounds that I open to see
everything that chains you
transformed into the green miracle
to take off the first layer
of the fence that separates us,
to think about collapse,
and if it's possible
to transfer something that heavy
into a tangible form:
wind, silk, girl,
leaves, blades,
cupboards, sparrow.

I will heal better,
learn how to swim through
this bloody tiredness
to breathe through the mirror
the round porthole you can find
everything there is in.
I am the embryo, the germ, the first cell
of an aquatic animal
enveloped in the embrace
of extraordinary beauty
which runs in the vessels of air,
the tawny throat
of an immense tide—
mud, mother
from which will emerge
a new me.

~ Cento of lines/phrases found in Frida Kahlo's diary and her letters.

Frida Kahlo's *Henry Ford Hospital (The Flying Bed)*, 1932

Frida, not everyone wants to see you unclothed on a hospital bed in the open air, industrial Detroit on the horizon, blood puddling beneath you. Clutched in your hand, long umbilical cords attached to floating objects: model of the female reproductive system, a snail, an orchid, your pelvis fractured in a bus accident when you were eighteen, and the male fetus you miscarried.

Miscarried, an odd word, *-mis* (wrongly)—to carry wrongly, as if you chose an incorrect way to carry your unborn son.

When shown in a New York exhibit six years later, your painting was titled *The Lost Desire.* I never desired to have children. People don't want to believe that. I've been told a marriage isn't valid unless it results in children. Schooled, as a preteen, by the faith I was raised in—procreation the only purpose for sex. Even then, I knew bullshit when I heard it.

This is a hard poem to write.
I wish your son had lived.

Frida, thirty years after your death, ecstatic to buy my first book of your art, a male clerk slid repulsed eyes over its cover, mouth squinched up like he'd bit into an extra sour lemon wedge. "I never cared for her," he stated, eyes lowered. I pretended not to hear his unwanted opinion. What I wanted was to slap his face, utter a few choice curses.

Frida Kahlo's *Memory,* 1937

I.

A sword, an arrow pierces her chest, heart absent, hunks of blue sky viewed through the open wound. Face rigid except for tears. Hair short, hacked off in response to another Diego betrayal, this time with her sister. Frida armless.

She straddles the coast. One foot in sea, the other in blood-soaked sand. Her massive heart—engorged aorta, vena cava, atrium, ventricle—plopped on the beach, drains, stains, in two ragged rivers of pain.

II.

A memory of my husband's last days in Hospice—his breaths soften as his lungs glut. I feel like the one suffocating—gulping myself back—my heart obscene as Frida's plump, exposed organ.

Frida Kahlo's *My Nurse and I,* 1937

I.

Infant with an adult head, held loosely, near falling from a wet nurse's arms—face covered by a dark mask, a grimace. Lush foliage reaches her shoulders.

Sky of raindrops mirrors two pearls of milk leaking like teardrops from the right breast. The left a translucent network, clusters of milk beads—tiny gold flowers.

Frida stares into space, empty. Doesn't suckle. The milk, dry stems, jabs her open mouth. Any minute she will choke.

II.

I open my mother's door, hold my breath. Her dread rivets me. She whimpers, tells me she dreamt the Book of Reckoning. Shows me how God's finger trailed down the page of all her sins. Says He revoked her voice, memory, control of her breathing.

Nothing I say penetrates. My throat throttled.

Frida Kahlo, *The Two Fridas,* 1939

A doubled self-portrait. Frida on the left wears white, the other rust and blue. Seated side by side, each holds a hand of the other, but their eyes never meet. Turbulent skies shift behind them. The Frida in white's chest is torn open, her heart broken, while the other's heart looms outside her body, but appears healthy. The heart-torn one bleeds badly, but tightens pincers around the blood vessel to staunch the flow. The hearts of both connect by arteries wound between them.

Isn't everyone twinned,
split in two, bifurcated,
whittling ourselves
down to one true self?

What You Dread

Memory. A chain
of collected jewels.
Endows, sings
your immense sadness.

Listen, use sudden beauty—
a soft kiss—to break
yourself against.

~ Found poem composed/modified from a list of words on p. 230 of *The Diary of Frida Kahlo,* translated by Barbara Crow de Toledo and Ricardo Pohlenz.

I'm Starting to Get Used to Suffering

I don't want to talk about wounds—
swollen bugs—spinning waves of pain
and immense sadness nothing can take away,
this traitor world, beloved monster,
always with me wherever I go—
a magenta stain.

There is always something new to see.
Give me the grace
to make an emulsion of beauty and hope
that impels me to paint
the caress of leaves becoming earth,
the purple quadrant of your faraway eyes–
mirrors of rapture—
verdigris, the embrace of time
that flies like a bullet.

I am eagerly awaiting
the subtle sting
of truth contained in the lies
at the border of collapse.

Can you imagine
a blossoming of the invisible,
a linking together
of me as yourself,
an internal lyric
that makes the world tremble?

~ Cento of lines/phrases found in Frida Kahlo's diary and her letters.

Frida Kahlo's *The Dream, (The Bed)*, 1940

A two-tiered bed rides a riotous sky. Frida sleeps below, a skeleton above. Both recline on their sides, face us, heads pressed on two pillows. The skeleton hugs a dead bouquet to its heart, legs skeined with dynamite, mouth a breach of barbed teeth.

Yes, life is rife with rancor and ruin. I dream of dying: high on a cliff edge, the car's front-heavy engine tips me into the canyon— nonstop velocity—my voice, breath snatched.

Frida, all the times you skirted death. Here, you paint yourself snugged under a blanket radiant as flames, safe in the embrace of a green vine, leaves so close you inhale their peppery zest.

Or is this your funeral pyre?

Frida Kahlo's *Self Portrait with Necklace of Thorns and Hummingbird*, 1940

Frida,

This may be my favorite of your self-portraits. You against a dense array of broad tropical leaves—your vast aura of veined green. A pair of pale blue butterflies land in the lacuna of your dark braids, echo two dragonflies that hover above you.

Behind one shoulder, a black spider monkey, behind the other a jaguar. I see them as protectors, not merely symbols of evil and bad luck. *They have your back.*

Yes, a few drops of blood dot your neck from your necklace of thorns, but it holds a hummingbird amulet I interpret as flight and hope. The necklace doubles as an embrace of stem and root from the foliage behind you—the clasp of growth.

Yes, you suffered incessant pain, thirty-five operations, some botched, years bedridden.

But I settle on your face, a heart at the center—calm, tenacious, unforgettable. Afloat in a hotbed of emerald.

Frida Kahlo's *The Broken Column*, 1944

I.

A crucifixion: eight nails puncture her face, six each arm, thirty-two in the rest of her torso. A spike pricks her heart. Split from the neck down, a ragged chasm reveals her severed spine—a vise all that pins her together.

Her chest echoed in the land—parched, deep crevices as when tectonic plates collide, fracture.

A sheet veils her lower body, as if to say, *enough. You've seen enough.* Polio as a child. Impaled by metal in a bus accident when a young adult. Endless trespasses endured: exams, surgeries, braces, casts, amputation.

Her eyes haunt me. The assault of her anguish.

II.

My mother's eyes plead. Confused, terrified, certain she won't survive until bedtime. I remind her she's depressed, the psychiatrist changed her meds, they take time to enter her system.

She won't, can't believe me. "You don't understand. I'm not going to get better. It's too late." Same words with her other two depressive episodes, before meds kicked in and she was herself again.

I distract her, talk her into playing a card game, something her true self loves, to occupy her hands and mind, let her face and eyes relax to what the doctor terms *flat, no expression.* Better than her terror, what she can't translate.

Her eyes rivet me, her eldest daughter, a grimace of *Why won't you help me?* A stare there's no way to answer.

There is so little known about

all this madness
the thirst of many years
the accumulated poison
in an urge to possess
subtle sting
of criminal silences
through millions of stone beings

what remains, are the transparent roots appearing
a return in time to that other time
quietly, the grief. Loudly, the pain
the slightest hope
will form the exact language for
the thread and the hair
the fingers of the wind
the caress of fabrics
the murmur of streams
the one who captures color
all the bells
trembling in the ticking
pulse of light

the same cloudy yellow sky
above all, the magnificent
the green-gold of your eyes
I have never seen tenderness as great
a doorway open to
the violence of being
inky worlds
still full of sensations
where shall I turn my eyes?

~ Cento of lines/phrases taken from *Frida Kahlo's Diary,* translated by Barbara Crow de Toledo and Ricardo Pohlenz.

Frida Kahlo's *Without Hope,* 1945

Bed exposed in a desert—earth deeply gouged, no water nor green, molten sun too near. Heavy linens pin her from the chest down. Above her an easel holds a massive funnel glutted with severed fish heads, plucked birds, a rope of plump sausage links, a whole pig, a skull, a long pelt ruptured. Everything raw, crammed between her lips. Tears on her cheeks, eyes savage, barbed.

Have you been force-fed
others' needs, expectations—
what women should be?

Frida Kahlo's *The Wounded Deer*, 1946

I.

Deer body smoothly fused into Frida's neck and head, antlers a tiara, a crown of thorns. One earring hangs like a tear from her furred ear. Caught mid-leap, trying to escape pain. Pierced by nine arrows, blood flows, the worst wound her heart.

Enveloped by bare trees, brittle skeletons with gashes of their own, blighted or struck by lightning, cores hollow.

Frida turns her face to us—defiant death mask. Tail tucked, all four feet off ground. The balmy blue of water and sky, no help. Bent legs so thin, soft underbelly pale. Beneath her, a torn branch, alive for only seconds longer.

II.

In Catholic grade school, I was given a holy card of the martyr St. Sebastian, tied to a tree. Neck, ribs, waist, groin, legs punctured with arrows, face contorted. I crushed it into a fist, flushed it down the toilet.

Colour is tangible

light as a child's kiss
magic, violent as new love

speaks truth if you listen
with your heart

when you paint colour
you feel form, grace

and sometimes silence
anguish, madness

~ Found poem composed/modified from Frida Kahlo's word list on p. 205 of *The Diary of Frida Kahlo,* translated by Barbara Crow de Toledo and Ricardo Pohlenz.

Frida Kahlo's *Tree of Hope,* 1946

Everything fractured. Sky split—the left, clouds and blue cradle sun; the right, pale moon looms in dense dark. Ground barren, a map of rivery fissures.

Two Fridas, one draped in a white sheet, inert on a gurney. Blood drips from wounds that echo deep earth crevices. Another blundered surgery. A second Frida clothed in red, free for the moment from a spinal brace that dangles from her hand.

So much pain depicted, yet she floats a flag lettered with hope.

Frida, did your paintings
soothe you, or bury you
further into trauma?

Inscription in *Frida Kahlo's Masterpieces,* Half Priced Books

for Lou

Inside: cramped letters inscribed on the title page, signed *Heath, January 9th*—the day my husband died fifteen years ago. Addressed to *Miyuki,* the words so familiar, in Lou's voice: *I am certain of nothing but the holiness of the heart's affection, and the truth of the imagination*—Keats from a letter to a friend. While *Bright Star* credits rolled, the actor recited "Ode to a Nightingale" in a whisper. Like John and Fanny, I imagine Heath and Miyuki lovers. He gave her the art book on their anniversary. But she never liked Frida's art; its rawness reminded Miyuki of botched love.

The pages virginal, turned by me only. I feel Heath's fervor buying the book, his joy as Miyuki rips speckled tissue, touches the cover, mouths the words inside—the only time she opens the book. On her cocktail table like an albatross—one more thing she never explores. But I want to linger on the moment she sees her lover's cursive, loops she follows across the page. I see her seated, eyes closed, palms pressed to Frida's face as Heath speaks the words he knows by heart.

Listen to Me

Nobody is separate
from anybody else
Here I am
in the womb of my
blooming in the joy of
hidden rhythms
on the lips of dreams
the window from where I
sharpened to the point of infinity
the words kept forming
a door in my imagination

~ Cento of lines/phrases taken from *Frida Kahlo's Diary,* translated by Barbara Crow de Toledo and Ricardo Pohlenz.

Frida Kahlo's *The Love Embrace of the Universe*, 1949

A triangle of connection,
nested Babushka dolls,

worlds to clasp: sun, moon, music,
art, words, dance, forests, lakes, loves—

never-ending realms within realms
to layer, seam, embroider our lives,

smother pain and fear,
purl us safe in intricate webs.

If only we can remember
the ways we are embraced:

the fervid green of soft moss,
violin, harp, and cello's liquid lilt,

pierce of lilac and lily-of-the-valley,
how water cradles us silky-thick.

Our first date—the tenor of your voice
as you sang to me—blue notes

tickling the plush dark.

I Have Wanted to Explain to You

Everything is upside down
nothing has a name
there is movement
which I shape into the space of my room
the tangible form
of what's enclosed in the belly
The immense tide
of the heart
the green miracle of my body
the one who gave birth to herself
not knowing that we are headed towards ourselves
I am the embryo, the germ, the first cell
wrapped in ancient roots

~ Cento of lines/phrases taken from *Frida Kahlo's Diary,* translated by Barbara Crow de Toledo and Ricardo Pohlenz.

Frida Kahlo's *Watermelons,* 1954

Your final painting, eight days before your death,
a still life of cut watermelons signed in large letters
on the pulp of one wedge: *Viva la Vida—Long Live Life.*

In pain from an amputated leg, you wrote
in your diary, *I hope the exit is joyful,*
and I hope never to return.

Your rinds deep emerald, medium green, chartreuse;
whole, halved, quartered, cut like a faceted flower,
each petal pointed. One slice studded with seeds.
Your crimson marrow—sweet, plump, fragrant salve.

Tell me if you're still learning

the living heart of the true
things that ignite life—
blue tenderness, yellow love
murmur of a stream's wave in your hand
a full moon, the lip of dreams
the inheritance you carry

You'll get lost on the way
in the regrettable condition of the world
separated by another wall
the accumulated poison of so much wealth
and so much poverty
one depends on the other
it's incredibly cruel
a terrible inflammation
pitch black like a wolf's mouth

But please be a little patient
This process is a doorway
the blissful border
to the entrails of the earth
the enormous spine, the deep roots
of the tree of hope
blooming in the joy
of the exact language for understanding

What secret are you looking for?
We are heading toward ourselves
This is the moment
Break the bark
Let new blossoms come out

~ Cento of lines/phrases found in Frida Kahlo's diary and her letters.

After Reading Frida's Letter to Georgia O'Keeffe, March 1, 1933

I thought of you a lot and never forget your wonderful hands and the color of your eyes. I will see you soon.
—Frida Kahlo

Frida, you met Georgia in New York, 1931. I
can only imagine, at 24, what you thought

of her, already renowned at 44. Both of
you married successful, unfaithful older men. You

experienced tumultuous marriages, shared a
passion for letter-writing, dressed in a lot

of striking ways: you, colorful, flamboyant, and
Georgia austere, but dramatic. Never

raised children though you longed to, Frida. I forget
how many of your pregnancies ended in miscarriage. Your

last—months away—plus your mother's death, yet how wonderful
that you called Georgia when she was confined to bed, hands

humming, saying how sorry you were to hear she felt poorly, and
when hospitalized, sent a kind letter, reminiscing about the

exquisite nature of Georgia's hands, and the unforgettable color
of her eyes, reported to be *speckled blue and brown*. Of

your handwriting, Frida—what a pleasure it is to see how your
hands formed the letters—careful, sweet, lovely as your dark eyes,

voluminous as speculation about whether you two had an affair. I found an intimate photo of you and singer Chavela Vargas. I will

never forget your beauty. White carnations frame your face. I see she wears a bud in her lapel buttonhole, and a thin bracelet—you

a wide one. Eyes closed with laughter, delight. *I will see you soon.*

II.

Scar Beauty, Inflame It

Georgia O'Keeffe
1887–1986

My first memory is of light—
the brightness of light—
light all around.

Here I am again

behind in my life, floundering
in an awful rut, so exquisitely raw
waiting for something to happen
like an alarm clock all wound up
ready to go off.
I'd like to paint the world
and I don't want to be careful.

The emptiness of the space
ahead is appalling
feeling around in the dark
in my nakedness.
Pieces of what I want to say
yanking at me,
a high pile of tumbleweeds
twisting in my mind
until, wading in this slime,
something boils over—

a kind of permanent shape
growing in meaning
a lush dream of vermillion
soft green, deep butter yellow
dirty lavender.

I feel like the wind
breathing so deep I'll break
so full I'm drunk
smothered with the pull
of the steep places,
kicking holes in the world
right through to the crust
of the earth, the hot part.

I am lost you know.
It's hell and I like it—
to work like a tiger
enjoying the muddle
the holiness.

~ Cento of lines/phrases found in Georgia O'Keeffe's letters.

Voluminous

The orifice consumes the frame
a vast, open mouth
molten

as if you ingested the sun
or spilled your candescence

tongue, a tide of fireballs

~ Inspired by Georgia O'Keeffe's painting *Special No. 21.*

Georgia O'Keeffe's *Blue No. 1,* 1916

Misshapen skulls float, wrinkly lobes
of cortex, cerebellum cased within.

Blue, pale to black—
brain moods.

A hundred-billion
creamy neurons flow.

Two parallel structures jut—
a ladder thrust diagonal, no rungs.

My mother's brain
misfires.

A network of endless
paths. No wonder
we sometimes get lost.

Georgia O'Keeffe's *Blue No. II,* Watercolor, 1916

Two blue ears float in an off-white bath—
echoes of each other. Lobes, royal blue

bleeding to paler tones, hints
of muddy teal and sea green, smudged

to imply muffled hearing.
Sinister, to see ears unattached.

Below, four parallel lines—diagonal slathers
same degression of blues, dark to light.

Are the lines soundwaves
traveling toward the ears?

Will the ears unspool
to make more linear streaks?

The four lines look furious
like words to burn ears.

The ears, placid. It takes care
to construct a curve.

Or are the ears fiddlehead ferns?
No, nautilus shells
destined for a slanted seabed.

Georgia O'Keeffe's *Nude Series VIII,* Watercolor, 1917

Her body vibrant blue and sea green
edges wavy, skin more porous
like a shore that fails to cinch
an ocean in place.
She sits cross-legged
in no visible chair
free-floats in chalk-white
except for one tiny brush poke

smudge above an elbow
calculated to convey
*Yes, there's power in my points
my hidden bones.*

Neither hands nor feet
but wide hips.
Her frame, planes of color
that overlap in darker patches.
One diagonal arm reaches
for something outside the frame.
The other touches her blank face.
Deep red throat and mouth—
her voice centers.
Where her heart, areolas,
and ovaries stow—golden pink.
Legs fused into a tail.
She's morphing back
into a water woman.

Georgia O'Keeffe's *Light Coming on the Plains III,* Watercolor, 1917

I.

The sun rises, vibrates
light into inky night

II.

A teal dome hovers above a disk. A horizon
separates the two—their negative space

III.

An earthenware vessel balanced
in a niche that holds it in place

IV.

A murky seashell opens to reveal
an opalescent, radiant orb

V.

You enter a dim cave
tiptoe toward pale blue

Georgia O'Keeffe's *Evening Star No. V*, 1917

I.

Volcanic Venus, a spiral unravels a long tail,
 consumes the deep blue tie-dyed sky.
Outlined in livid white—negative space.

II.

A red eyelid cradles a yellow eyeball.

III.

Gyre of fire. Centrifuge.

IV.

In a heavy bowl, an egg yolk.

V.

Molten nugget of gold cinched
by an incandescent wrench.

VI.

Color of the chest-high metal cabinet
glutted with tools my husband inherited
from his father, a bus mechanic.
Now, left for me.

When I slide open the drawers,
tinny clink of steel against steel, like bells,
lustrous silver, cool to my fingertips,
silky as creek water.

Georgia O'Keeffe's *Special #12*, 1917

I.

Spiral iterations
interlocked waves
one behind the other
stand upright like a cobra
ready to strike

II.

A fern uncurling open
from its braided base

III.

A doorknob turning
in a man's hand

IV.

A lock of wet hair
around an earlobe

V.

The handle of an antique cane
the black-lacquered wooden one
my husband owned
that I don't remember him using
thin, like it wouldn't hold you

VI.

The cane I needed
after a knee replacement
still in my trunk a year later

VII.

The entwined selves:
childhood, furthest away
only an edge visible
pale, not yet formed

The middle murky, almost blank
center, still becoming

Closest, dark and thin
nearly replete, loops back
plush with inky beauty

Georgia O'Keeffe's *Blue and Green Music,* 1919

I.

A progression:
sound as ocean waves
lunge from the bottom
evolve ever longer
as they surge
toward center

Slanted green, black blades
plummet, meet in a vee
frame a strange flower
petals separate, open
in a convex curve
seaweed swaying

II.

Sharp knives slice
a cross section
wedge of cabbage
so crisp you can taste it

III.

Bodies vibrate, arch
cadenced ecstasy
arms raised
like flames

Georgia O'Keeffe's *Series I, No. 8, 1919*

I.

Green apple split top to bottom
encapsulated in a blue severed heart

hugged by rhythmic pink pulmonary vessels
clasping lung sacs—twin bellows

Will the halved mirror images
stitch the fissures whole?

II.

My parents, first husband,
all emphysema.

Second one,
lung cancer.

Me as a child, asthma,
inhaler hidden—my secret defect.

Today I want to paint nakedness

to put on paper anything I choose
to satisfy a fine kind of hunger.
What is it I want to say?
My ideas are still in a liquid state
forming blue shadows.
Isn't dark curious, enormous, intangible?
Sometimes it chases you.
I feel like beefsteak broiled
not done in the middle,
my mind ravenous
the lid on a boiling kettle.
Everything contradicts the other
uprooting, twisting and turning.

I want to paint a woman
with nothing on but her skin
so damnably free
without the weight
a trembling kind of sweetness
untouchable, soft and feathery,
all water colors, stretched out
intensely alive—
a bigness that carries me away
an explosion I've been growing to all my life.

I'm beginning to realize
what seeing means.
Being so afraid makes it all the finer,
a kind of balance
headed for something
more feeling than brain—
the world softening
like green moss.

~ Cento of lines/phrases found in *My Faraway One: Selected Letters of Georgia O'Keeffe and Alfred Stieglitz: Volume One, 1915–1933.*

Georgia O'Keeffe's *Red and Orange Streak,* 1919

I.

Against black sky
a red horizon
wavy on top
like painted hills
in the distance

A wide streak arcs a flame
orange, yellow, olive-green
from earth to sky
opposite of lightning

A cloud, or is it smoke, hovers
under the slanted span
feathered, hazy
a patch of moss

II.

Trajectory of a bullet
blood vessel eviscerated
flatline on a monitor

III.

Curved beak
a sword-billed hummingbird
scarlet tongue flicking

IV.

A vault of paint
slung into the dark

V.

Intersecting orbits
two heavenly bodies
and a new, veiled nebula

Georgia O'Keeffe's *Zinnias,* 1921

White, soft pink, raspberry
painted against pale, dreamy blue

Fuzzy, as if viewed through
wavy glass or a glare of sun

Edges rounded, except
for a green stem, a leaf blade

Sex organs flecked yellow at the center
One zinnia's lower petals a silvery array

of mini curved moons starting
their spent descent to earth

Sweet blear of summer heat
how objects look when you fall asleep

fluid, as you slip into the dream
where your husband returns to life

body no longer scarred, lungs unhampered
spine perfectly aligned, lips supple plums

And you wake, a sweet-bitter
tang on your tongue

as if you'd bitten
into plush, heady petals

Georgia O'Keeffe's *Lake George with Crows,* 1921

I.

At the spire of the world, Crow Mother surveys the Trinity of creation: Heaven, Water, Earth. Her three sons glide, wings wide, in an arc over the azure oval framed by a rim of brown mountain and a blur of turning trees—dark, pale, crimson. In a thin strip of ashen sky, a long cloud bisects a creamy full moon. It's dusk. The black triad heads to their night roost.

II.

A Cooper's hawk leaves a junco's torn feathers, strings of intestines in snow by my patio. Seconds later, a crow swoops, guzzles the remains, every drop of blood—the white once again pristine.

Georgia O'Keeffe's *Pattern of Leaves or Leaf Motif #3*, 1923–4

I.

They fill the frame, intense, close as a palm raised to your face. Deeply veined. Collage of layers. Background smoke. Three leaves overlaid, one on another.

Bottom one, only ruffled edges—a gray-green shadow. Middle leaf, white as if furred with mold. The top dark maple the color of merlot, in places almost black like dried blood. A vertical cut clean through the pulp, zigzag of lighting strike. Yellow in the wound. Break of sunlight. Exquisite. Obscene. A plump heart yanked from a body.

II.

A torn heart.

III.

The slash so clean hints leafcutter ants. Voracious hunger that consumes in minutes. Flesh-eating driver ants in *The Poisonwood Bible*. A village runs for the river.

IV.

Is it hard to paint violence? To form that jagged gash, nearly disconnect one half from the other? To scar beauty. Inflame it.

Georgia O'Keeffe's *New York with Moon*, 1925

The edge of a dusking city, workday's end
I idle under a red stoplight

hemmed in by slick monoliths
bronze, copper clasping remnants of sun

A low church, spire
soaked in orange

Still blue, the wedged sky
a lopsided arrow

Moon tucked in slanted, layered
waves of clouds

Suspended on a black pole, a streetlamp
shaped like a heart, haloed by a large aura

Headed to meet a new love
for a river walk, a late dinner

I wait, mesmerized by the pale orb
the crimson signal, and in between

the furry corona circles
the lit lamp so like a heart

Georgia O'Keeffe's *Red and Brown Leaves,* 1925

I.

Cloudy, primal green floods
the canvas, superimposed
with a scarlet maple
and sepia poplar leaf
upright as rooted trunks.
A trinity—three seasons—
death closest.

II.

Stages of cancer—yours
when found near Easter.
You died in the height
of fall. Everywhere the stab
of color, the crunch underfoot,
the must of decay. Even weeds
along the freeway translated
to beauty, all repellent.

Georgia O'Keeffe's *The Old Maple, Lake George, 1926*

Wide shoulders reach—
massive branches
lopped off by the frame

Jarringly close, the maple
gobbles the canvas, cropped
so only the thick middle visible

Gray bark deeply rutted
knotted, rotted hollow

Like exposed organs
large burls scar the trunk

One lean branch twists
into a forked hook, a "Y" formed

Another, a crooked elbow
balances a "V" on top

Two cavities, gaping mouths—
portals to inner darkness

How many rested, nested here
how many still burrow in its furrows?

Georgia O'Keeffe's *The Lawrence Tree,* 1929

I.

Against electric blue
night sky, star-speckled
clumped black foliage
from terracotta trunk
rises beyond the painting
no earth in sight
free-floating in space

II.

Trunk diagonal
as seen from below
falls toward you
like a magnet
pulls you
into its branches

III.

An exposed spinal column
and ancillary nerves flow parallel—
femoral, sacral, phrenic,
pudendal, ulnar, cervical,
radial, intercostal—a litany
to tickle the tongue

IV.

African giant millipede
fifteen inches long
two hundred fifty legs
secretes acid from its pores
clouds of black poison

V.

In ocean floor silt
blood worm, fire worm
equipped with fleshy spurs
stinging barbs

VI.

Mutant, multi-armed cephalopod
jets an orgy
of dark ink
into the blue, blue sea

Georgia O'Keeffe's *At the Rodeo, New Mexico, 1929*

I.

Circles within circles:
red, brown, mustard, green, blue—
multiple eyelids—tiny pupil,
scarlet iris with feathered edges
radiates waves of pink,
yellow, aqua blood vessels
that triangulate the white.

II.

A camera lens: interlocking
rings to adjust your view.

III.

Hypnotic, dizzying.

IV.

My first and only time
at Florence Speedway,
car races on a dirt track:
stink of gas, oil, rubber,
metallic as the taste of blood,
air curdled with dust and smoke,
the contagion of excitement,

revved-up engines goosebumped
my husband, but scalded my ears,
thwacked my chest—
the volume an intensity,
a dense weight
I couldn't contain.

Georgia O'Keeffe's *Jack-in-the-Pulpit II,* 1930

Succulent green leaves swaddle
one flower: dark garnet—the color
of red beets, merlot, an eggplant's skin,
dried blood—garish against white veins
that flow, thin rivers. A purplish club rises
like a phallus from the striped hood.

Magnified so close, it unnerves,
reminds me of dark
slippery organs
that terrified me as a child.
I tried not to imagine them
hunkered beneath my skin.

Georgia O'Keeffe's *Summer Days,* 1936

I.

Massive skull hovers high in a smoke-white sky above a rippling line of copper-colored sand hills. Dark cavities cradle eyes, a line lengthwise bisects the tapering muzzle. Magnificent antlers fork, two trinities. A god ascends to a throne in the afterlife. Below, yellow and red desert flowers, a ritual offering.

II.

Under an oak tree, a jawbone we name *coyote* or *lynx*—the words exotic, risky. We bury its two long canines on a creek island, place Queen Anne's lace over dirt we stamp, our soles molding puzzle patterns. Imagine the teeth, seeds to sprout full-grown mammals come spring. They'll slink from slumber dens—hissing, howling to their clan.

Georgia O'Keeffe's *Two Jimson Weeds,* 1938

Nightshade. Blossoms highly magnified,
inches from your face, disorient.

Curvy leaves stink. White, pleated petals unspiral,
scent mesmerizing. Sometimes toxic if ingested.

Multiply-named *angel trumpet, moonflower,
thornapple, devil's cucumber.*

Blooms at night, sipped by moths, vital
in witches' brews. An aphrodisiac in India.

Ancient tribes used for epilepsy, asthma,
to induce visions, lessen pain when setting bones.

Spiny four-chambered capsules packed with seeds
lie dormant for years, sprout when disturbed.

The summer before we moved,
two years before my husband died,

we grew the rampant vine in a square
hemmed by house and driveway.

He cut a ten-inch tubular bud, floated it
in cool water, to unfurl inside at dusk.

If only I'd saved some seeds.

Georgia O'Keeffe's *Dead Cottonwood Tree, Abiquiu,* 1943

Sky suffused lilac-blue.
Behind the dead tree
a line of live ones,
curry-yellow foliage
feverish as flames.

Smooth, bone-white trunk
picked-clean, desert-baked.
Wide base, an onion bulb
peeling layers charred by lightning,
black thorn in its side.

Long wounds,
a hollow core.
One branch remains,
split open lengthwise,
reaching beyond the frame.

O, tribal elder,
risen goddess,
may we embrace
our scars,
may we all be
as dazzling,
nude.

Is It True?

*I've been absolutely terrified every minute of my life—and I've
never let it keep me from doing a single thing I wanted to do.*
—Georgia O'Keeffe, at 99

Georgia, but what about your macular degeneration? I've
read that at age 77, you already had trouble seeing. I've been

diagnosed with the disease at 63 which absolutely
crushed me. My mother in her mid-80's was terrified

to discover, by accident, she'd lost every
sliver of forward vision in her left eye. In a quick minute,

learned she was half blind. Her right one assumed the job of
seeing for both eyes, compensating. When I learned my

eyes held *the seeds,* and though they might not ripen, my life
derailed. Avid movie-goer, photographer, reader, and

writer, losing my vision felt like the worst possible fate. I've
let it go, take special vitamins, weekly self-tests, hope it never

develops further. Georgia, what about when your doctor let
you know, to recover from nervous exhaustion, it

was vital you not paint for a year. Did you keep
that prescription for recovery? Me—

I don't believe I could live a year without writing. From
1972 on, you could not paint unassisted, doing

everything with only slight peripheral sight. A
shock that must have been. Yet you had a single-

minded view—a passion to continue—a thing
you couldn't abandon. So, you worked with clay. I

read that at 85 you hired a 27-year-old assistant; you wanted
to still create. I imagine you feeling your way into shapes, to

remake beauty with your hands and heart. What else can we do?

Georgia O'Keeffe's *Pelvis III,* 1944

The bleached pelvis devours the frame. Raised to sky, a telescope, the blue blooms through the bone hole, breach calves birth through. Imagine how its hooves pounded earth, in glee, terror.

Or a soft-shelled robin's egg, just laid, hoarded in a hollow of white sand?

Oval balm
Form within form
A nesting.

Ten years old, near an abandoned stone barn, the skeletal head of a fox. Sharp teeth intact in pointed snout. I place fingers in a nasal cavity, an eye socket, where ears once sensed mice stir in a burrow, rabbits rustle grass. Feel inside its jaw for the missing, sinewy tongue.

An ache thrums my throat
Grief for all the absent ones
Hum of connection.

Georgia O'Keeffe's *It Was Red and Pink,* 1959

Yin and yang.
Pink—girly.
Red—Power,
color of fire, blood, the root chakra,
cherries, traffic lights, stop signs,
Little Red Riding's hood,
matador's cape,
cupid and devil,
love and hate,
a flushed face,
Scarlet Letter shame.

The red pantsuit Mom forbid me
to buy, *Wearing red turns heads.*
Amsterdam's sex district,
luck in China, what brides wear,
mourning in Africa.

As if the artist poured paint
let it drift, imprint,
before she dipped brush
in water, wet the canvas,
strew suffused, unfurled pigments
mud-brown, marbly-green.

Tall, red cannas lined the length
of my husband's house.
Tender perennials, he unearthed them
each fall to replant in spring.
When we moved to a condo
we gave the knotted rhizomes
to my sister. Did they survive him?

I remember he said, *Bury them*
with their eyes face up.

Georgia O'Keeffe's *It Was Blue and Green,* 1960

I.

A smudged, sand landscape
viewed from above.

Clear azure
outlined by, or shadowed in,
sea-green, almost mint,
thrust like a tongue
into pure white—
a desert river delta.

Two thin tributaries,
one with a runnel of its own,
bleed out
thin rivulets,
delineate land masses
into puzzle pieces.

II.

Desert snakes sidewind sand
undulate, luxuriate
in flagrant white heat.

The thick one yearns
to form a circle,
turns backward—
an ouroboros,
dying
to consume itself.

Living Is Such a Tangle

I felt quite thorny, full of wheels
and empty spots, limp from looking
over the edge, a battlefield terribly torn.
I made up my mind to try my own cure
but I couldn't go into it broken.

The world hurts, too many folks taking
pieces of me. I am here and I am not here,
a shell with a floating middle. I need
to breathe in my own way, get out
where the world is big and quiet.

I want to paint rich saturated pigments,
a language of line, a breathing
color reaching for violet and purple.
I want to paint fat-looking fig trees,
a lush soft green feel of birds,
a sweet stillness warm pink and lavender,
the Rio Grande River running
red from rains, bulging
out of the canvas.

Something is happening in me.
I am beginning to feel
as if I have dozens of selves,
all creation going through me
unfolding, blossoming—
a sled tearing downhill,
a piece of fast-burning wood.

But I am only a scrap,
little more than a thread
of the circle that nothing can break,
the desert stretching on and on
like the ocean, dark. Maybe blackness
is the pure thing after all—
the thing you cannot soil.

~ Cento of lines/phrases found in *My Faraway One: Selected Letters of Georgia O'Keeffe and Alfred Stieglitz: Volume One, 1915–1933.*

III.

Wild Convergence

Emily Carr
1871–1945

*Something has called out of somewhere
and something in me is trying to answer.*

When one is listening intensely

in the soft blackness of the night
heavily veiled in mystery
the remembrance garden deep in my heart
there is so much to feel
perhaps prayer is like that
the seething inside
too full of living to be written down
It's wanting keeps us going
like a wrong key turning round and round in a lock
It's all the unwordable things one wants
and having nothing happen

Life is full of opposite contraries
the freedom of memory and imagining
a longing to know and understand
so that nothing is lost
that makes the skin of you
feel like something namelessly exquisite
there is a lonely, blue brooding over everything
always unfolding, never in a hurry

I am circled by trees
moss, very deep and silent
the creatures are all folded down in sleep
the holy ones
guarding their precious secrets
a sky quivering with movement
glimpses of the between places

~ Cento of lines/phrases taken from *Hundreds and Thousands, The Journals of Emily Carr.*

Emily Carr's *War Canoes, Alert Bay,* 1912

Three canoes lodged on the sand beach
of Kwakwaka'wakw Village, Vancouver Island,

each carved from a single log of red cedar,
cormorants painted on the high prows

in purple, green, orange, blue—
colors echoed from sea, sky, trees,

mountains in the background.
Not only used for war, but to hunt, fish,

travel, transport and trade.
What did these indigenous people think

of this white woman painting
their history? Did they still stoke

the hope of reclaiming stolen lands?

Emily Carr's *Totem Mother, Kitwancool,* 1928

Totem within totem,
mother and child,

one the mirror of the other.
Mother makes a cradle of her body,

baby hugged against her chest,
one palm caps its head,

the other braces its feet,
torso papoosed by muscled arms.

Heads squared, amplified,
eyes bulged to snare skulkers.

Their aged wood burnished bronze.
The mother's knees rubbed raw;

her lips stretched wide—
a clamp of bliss, grit, ache.

Emily Carr's *The Great Eagle, Skidegate, B.C.,* 1929

His spiritual conception he buried deep in the woods he was about to carve.
—Emily Carr, *Growing Pains*

Everything pointed, sharp: towering
totem cocooned in a glass sky

shattered into a puzzle of prisms,
the firs' barbed crowns,

the eagle's beak, wing tips, staccato
slap of flying, the shredding talons

not visible. Cedar aged a rich bronze
and steel-blue as if morphing into sky,

petrifying. Large eyes deep-set,
mouth a wide grimace.

From his perch he scans all creation, face
in shadow, an intense tilt to his head.

Has he spotted prey, ready to lunge
and stab, or does he stare in disgust

at what the world's become?

Emily Carr's Untitled *[Eye in the Forest]*, 1929–30, Charcoal on Paper

Snarl of jarring forms,
light and dark
tangle of spiked pines,
triangular bites seized from their sides.

Curve of an ear, nose, beak,
a forked, reptilian tongue,
two mismatched eyes,
one pupil four times the size of the other,
a spiral unraveling from its socket.

A crazed raven totem
overgrown by the ravenous forest
it was culled from.

Emily Carr's *Zunoqua of the Cat Village,* 1931

Totem of an ogress, snakes for hair
hung on each side of her head
ready to nip her shoulders.

Large forehead, eyes ebony, empty,
mouth spread in a screech.

Said to steal and eat children
but also bring wealth.

Behind her a torrent
filled with cats drowning
in green, only their heads visible,
faces choked with wild eyes,
trapped between the ogress
and two buildings consumed
by swollen fire.

In the foreground, a lynx,
and a boar charges
from under a wave's belly.

A dark forest edges the background.
In the pine's murky understory
eyes loom.

Emily Carr's *Big Raven,* 1931

Matte, sooty black totem
faint mimic of live raven shine
base rooted in earth, wings clasp its side
but still I feel the crisp wingbeat cut air
the caw echo

Sky massive plates of vertical glass
prisms emanating
frosted blue, white, pink, yellow, green

Pine tree tangle of needled edges,
a distant brown mountain,
waves of green swirl like a flood, a fire
lick, lap, soon to tickle
singe its wings

Head high, jaw rigid
he oversees the world—
his stained, tainted creation.

To Wrestle Something Out for Myself

Something in me is trying to answer
the shapes of the trees
mountain cradling the cloud
reflected in the water
glorious cold green
a clearer language
a new delineation
a swing to the earth and sky

~ Cento of lines/phrases taken from *Hundreds and Thousands, The Journals of Emily Carr.*

Emily Carr's *Forest, British Columbia,* 1931–2

I.

No sky. Nothing but smothering
succession. Parallel tree trunks
linked parts of a whole, a schema, flow.
Braided tangle of foliage
heavy, creased curtains that block the way
green waves of oceans thrust
a final tsunami to bury the world

II.

Three-fourths up the crush
a sliver of golden light illumines
what it squeezes between

III.

No place for a foothold.
A few trunks hold spikes—
remnant of branches—
that will pierce skin

IV.

Cloy of soil, corroding wood, dense vegetation—
huddling confluences

V.

What you can't smell or see, but hear
burrow, rustle, plummet through air
sounds you can't pinpoint what direction
they come from. Everything echoes

VI.

Is that you breathing?

Emily Carr's *Gray,* 1931–32

Dense layers of dark forest
rise like spires, converge.
Deep color, the oldest trees, at the edges
less intense, young ones, near the center.

Nested one inside the other
branch and foliage in thick tents
flaps open to reveal
an illuminated seedling

cocooned in a pearly veil.
Igneous light divulges
a path, a passage out
past the beating heart.

Emily Carr's *Abstract Tree Forms,* 1931–32

I.

Sinuous waves of gold, green,
blue, orange, black—stacked
one upon another, high
as a cathedral—
accruing, ruthless
motion.

II.

You're lost
in the forest.
Evening approaches. Everywhere
trees packed close, canopies
and roots twined—an inseparable,
gravid mass. You could suffocate,
drown, in the cloying musk
of growth and decay.
Will you be braided
into the snarl?

Emily Carr's *Scorned as Timber, Beloved of the Sky,* 1932–35

Ninety percent sky over rolling hills
dotted with squat growth
dark green, charred black,
blue of mountain, maybe sea.

Three parallel spindly trees
bare except for tufts of apex foliage,
each trunk shorter by half, thinner
than the one to its left,
the tallest near the scene's ceiling.

Rejected by loggers. Diseased?
No room on the truckbed? Markers—
where workers left off, of the hacked
splendor, the heft of their theft.

Behind the *beloved* trio, arced discs
vibrate outward in waves—
the trees' radiance, or clouds, or smoke?
The rings closest to earth rise
dark as dregs of ruin.

One wonders how long these three, so exposed,
will stand, and if the greed of roots
can hold all that height.

Emily Carr's *Wood Interior,* 1932–35

No sky. Deep shade. Tall trees, tops lopped. Bowed trunks striated blue, gray, brown, flecks of silver and gold from sun or moonlight. Bare but for two high, spindly branches reaching.

The forest floor, green waves threaded with turquoise and ginger, lick the trunks like flames or floodwaters.

Near, thicker trees frame thin, distant ones that look like bars to hold back arced layers of dark rainbows—a whirling cataclysm, exquisite and awful. Not for the claustrophobic.

Two narrow yellow crescents whisper an opening, a path forward. How far would you sink, and what snakes slink in the deep green?

I Want to Have My Share

With their blind eyes
how does the seed
wait and listen
the memory of
a glowing pool of pure light
an answer to a great longing

There is a holiness
chords way down in my being
one great cone filled with
a joyfulness that catches you up
to give vibration
a surging through

Yet I am afraid
the sky is dark and wild

~ Cento of lines/phrases taken from *Hundreds and Thousands, The Journals of Emily Carr.*

Emily Carr's *Forest Interior in Shafts of Light,* 1935–37

Abstract dark, dense
muddy browns and greens
pierced with gold. A wide swath
of chartreuse, saffron, ginger streams
across the ground, a waterfall, long
hair combed to reveal
luster of individual strands.
From a tiny patch of azure a lightning bolt
zigzags, splits the scene with radiance.

O, to immerse in wild convergence,
what Japanese call *forest-bathing,*

gaze into towering crowns, touch hemlock,
Douglas fir, red cedar, taste spongy soil,
air aglut with fragrant needles,
swish of sway, scuttle of squirrel, flap
of wings. The nape of your neck prickles—
a lynx, red fox, timber wolf
unseen, near.

O, to step into
that aisle of light,
whelm in that gleam.

Emily Carr's *Reforestation,* 1936

I.

Below sky's spiral of blue and purple, green
gluts the canvas: emerald mountain firs,

a swath of pines quakes crystal gold
with sunlight, and thick heaves

of kelly-green grasses swamp
the valley once razed by fire, leveled

by loggers. From a shallow depression,
four spindly seedlings rise.

II.

I can't help but worry about the current wild-
fires. Every year, the US Forest Service states

an average of seven million acres burns. Yes,
this earth, this universe, teeters in continual flux.

One thing dies, another births.
Have we skewed the balance irrevocably?

Emily Carr's *Roots,* 1937–39

Nothing is dead, not even a corpse. It moves into the elements.
   —Emily Carr, Hundreds and Thousands

This dim-lit forest is no place for a pensive stroll. The ground a torrent of green and gold, a rhinoceros tusk rises from the broil. Seized in the nucleus of a cataclysm, trees convulse, twirl on their axes. A mammoth gnarled stump, heartwood rotted, thuds from its deep crater. Ripped, ragged roots mutate to a wild boar, a fire-breathing dragon; no, a snaggletooth shark erupting from its lair.

A snapshot of time
in a primeval forest
hulking upheaval

Emily Carr's *Sombreness Sunlit,* 1938–40

Sky, trees bathed
in horizontal sun-stripes
wave after thick wave
running contrary
to the forest floor
the ground holding
the weight of all
that radiance.

In the foreground, the lower trunks
break into bands of glow.
Whole sections of distant
thinner trunks obscured.
In the center, one tree bends
genuflecting or collapsing.

The longer you look
you realize trees are twirling
in place so fast
you can barely detect
their motion
the entire forest
a live vortex
a torrent of orbit
rings of ecstasy
spiraling
against the damp mass
of nearing night.

I Want So Terribly to Feel

If I knew where to find
a door into unknown
tranquil spaces filled with light
to feed on the silence and wonder
the quiet green ravines
the blue sea lapping them

The trees are heavy with it
such volume of glorious sounds
rhythm and space
voices in an unknown tongue:
We are still here
You are one of us

~ Cento of lines/phrases taken from *Hundreds and Thousands, The Journals of Emily Carr.*

Emily Carr's *Laughing Forest,* 1939

Orange, red, green trees
veined with yellow, gold

vibrate, shake as with a lavish belly-laugh
that resonates in waves

like wind, like water on shore
the quiver of being

growth to death to rot
nourishing the next birth

the ground, the sky, everything between
caught in the trembling net

Emily Carr's *Self-Portrait,* 1938–39

To paint a self-portrait should teach one something about oneself.
—Emily Carr, *Hundreds and Thousands*

                      You blend in
                                gray, green, black, brown
no boundary between you and   your chest wall and
what frames you   roughhewn wood panels
a massive trunk   beloved tree
            sun from a window, golden soup

The silver rim of your glasses   streaked locks near your ear
head turned to face us   mouth a closed line
eyes glare   a dare

You painted thick strokes   bands of color
angry, in a hurry   to suggest motion
the lash   of wild woods

In our mid-sixties, you and I   barrel-bodied, extra padded
You'll die in six years   so much left to paint
            time like the clamp of your jaw

                Did you, will I, ever learn
                self-kindness

What Is It You Are Struggling For?

Beauty: music that makes holes
in the sky; some unnamable thing?
Living things clamour
to be fed. I'm balancing
on the edge of a thread
of kindness. I want to love
as hard as I can.

I have wasted the years
waiting on corners in fog
because I was afraid
to wrestle something
out of myself. It is so hard
to keep from being choked
and swallowed up. The world
is a mean, sneaking place.
We've fouled it all.

I must empty myself
in the inky darkness
the quiet space of opening,
become a channel
for the pouring through.
I must go deeper
into the unvarnished me,
paint below the skin.

When I am through with this body—
little bundle of wreckage—
I want to swirl into deep, rich blue
holy places: a great river rushing
mountain cradling the cloud
hanging in the soft pleasant light
following the shapes of trees
humming among the leaves
in an unknown tongue
nurtured by the myriad of fallen
seeds expanding
each one knowing what to do—
dreams shaping themselves
in purified abandon.

~ Cento of lines/phrases found in *Hundred and Thousands, The Journals of Emily Carr.*

The enormous spine of the imagination

gives you a starting point, pith or kernel
a dream shaping itself
the window from where
I smell rain on the sages
see a beautiful grove of cottonwood trees
clouds making big dark shadows on the flatness
the sharp line of a storm
What language do they speak?

I am preparing a stew
of silence and wonder
quiet green ravines
the domed blue above, the friendly reds
bird noises and singing things
stars that touch the center of me
old scars, still tender
a shrinking sort of fear

I'm feeling sixty miles an hour
in soft, tired twinklings
it is beautiful and exhausting
as if I had straddled the whole world
to tell you about the music of it
great bundles of contradiction
with a hurt all through it
But light is thrown at it, time and attention
singing through the madness
a cellular arrangement
the trees are heavy with it

I am trying to see further
lead from joy back to mystery
There is never anyone to ask the things we most need to ask
Please tell me
do you feel like flowers sometimes—
little blue petals?
I hope so

~ Cento of lines/phrases found in the writings of Frida Kahlo, Georgia O'Keeffe, and Emily Carr.

About the Author

Karen George is author of five chapbooks, and three poetry collections from Dos Madres Press: *Swim Your Way Back* (2014), *A Map and One Year* (2018), and *Where Wind Tastes Like Pears* (2021). She won *Slippery Elm's* 2022 Poetry Contest, and her short story collection, *How We Fracture,* which won the Rosemary Daniell Fiction Prize, was released from Minerva Rising Press in January 2024. She is the recipient of grants from Kentucky Foundation for Women and Kentucky Arts Council and earned an MFA in Writing from the Sena Jeter Naslund-Karen Mann Graduate School of Writing. Her work appears in *Adirondack Review, Valparaiso Poetry Review, Cultural Daily, Atticus Review, The Ekphrastic Review,* and *MacQueen's Quinterly.* She retired from a career as a computer programmer/analyst to write full-time. She lives in Florence, Kentucky, enjoys photography and visiting museums, forests, cemeteries, historic towns, and bodies of water.

Visit her website at:
karenlgeorge.blogspot.com